47....

and counting

MINKA WILTZ

BookLeaf Publishing

India | USA | UK

Made with ♥ on the BookLeaf Publishing Platform

www.bookleafpub.in

www.bookleafpub.com

*To my past 47 years on this planet, in this body.
To the baby who learned to focus her eyes in the
harsh light of the illusion, we call reality.*

*To the little girl who tried to cook her single
mother a chicken dinner on a gas stove and
singed her hair.*

*To the teenager who believed in the rogue
religiosity and pain of her mother.*

*To the twenty-year-old who threw herself into
beds with strangers to find answers to unwritten
mysteries.*

*To the thirty-year-old who loved the wrong
people to birth two perfect children.*

*To the forty-year-old who finally stopped trying
to 'get it right,' then 'got it wrong', learned how to
be loved, be at peace while she healed.*

*To all of my selves, and the bumps, bruises, scar
tissue, and knowledge. Now you are ready to
change the world and choose your inner circle
more wisely. I dedicate this book to you.*

We're just getting started.

Acknowledgment

Anjoli. You are a light! Thank you for being in my life.

Christopher Meadows, for being a loving force.

Katrina Marie, for teaching me how to heal.

Pecola Dumas Odum, Johnny Odum, Patricia Odum, Phoebe Odum. Your family has been my support net since I was six weeks old. There would have to be an entire book dedicated to my gratitude for your kindness. Love beyond measure to you all!

To Phyllis Smith! You have taught me to stand up for myself in ways no one has before. A Mama Bear! Love to you always!

To the Sexton Family, thank you for your love and support.

Arnab "Pom" for having been there.

Max, for inspiring me by example. You are my first SuperHero!

Tangelique for being such a loving constant in my world.

Angela, for being you.

Lynne, for cheering me on, pouring love into my soul and supporting my family with your love and presence.

Mikki, for your love and unswerving encouragement.

Beth Christie. There are so many years—40, I believe. Through them all, you have been a Whyte Southern/Brooklyn Woman I can trust. LMAO!

Wolff—your friendship has been reassuring in this new place.

Sparky! Love you, dear friend

To Mama and Daddy—Olivia and George, you got me here, and now I gotta do my part. Love to you both. I feel you near me. Thank you.

This is just the first book! I've got more of my village to thank in the next one!

Preface

My early years as a singer and actor were filled with the pressure and anticipation from others for me to "become famous". That hasn't happened and it probably won't. The idea of being fish-bowled everywhere I go is not exciting to me. (Then again, we are all under surveillance, so I guess that is inevitable for all of us).

I have always been more interested in learning from brilliant people who create beautiful worlds in unexpected ways. Right now, the singer Iniko comes to mind. Such a marvellous talent and visionary ET!

Writing has been a welcome solitude. I get to hide in delectable worlds of my own creation. In cozy solitude.

When I came up with the idea to write these poems, I was two weeks into my forty-seventh year on this planet. The world around me seemed poised to explode with new chaos brewing daily and, somehow, I felt grateful to be alive to witness it. At forty-seven years old, this is the first time in my life when I actually feel real love for myself. With real love comes strength and healing. With strength and healing comes a renewed sense of purpose. Finally, my life holds meaning for me.

The words in this book are sent out as a beacon calling out to your purpose and strength. A beacon to your love and healing. It's there! Be still and let it rise to the surface. Maybe you will be inspired to sing your own song or write your own story.!
Whatever you do, don't give up on YOU! Sending pure love!

Do you feel it?

-Minka Wiltz
minkawiltz.com

FEROCIOUS

IT'S FEROCIOUS

this feeling deep inside of me
before morning has broken

i know you will leave

when the stars retreat
and the sun shines in on me

it's only natural
you are free

MOMENTS

You are not my ally
Not my enemy
You are one moment in eternity
Still I feel the warmth of your body next to
mine
Because we crave closeness
We are
garish
hurtful
stunning
Human and so much more
Truth tears away at me
It calls to my soul

There is more to existence
than validation from another
Truth is my frightening mistress
If I ignore her
maybe she will be no more
and the burden of purpose
will be forgotten
We are cloaked in distractions
Mind-numbing moments meant
to help us forget
Our power
and loneliness together

ROYALTY

A Queen rushes toward me
The skirts of her gown
gathered in her hands

I stand still–free
Knowing I rush for no one

The flesh that is hers
exists because of mine

Jewels as chains
around her neck
My existence is divine
in the presence of depravity

LOVE GOT ME INTO

Not a preacher man
Nobody's saint

He was more than a sinner

Not a gentleman unless
You closed your eyes and let him in

My eyes were open
The whole time I was grinning

My eyes never closed
Even when my head was spinning

What has Love got Me into this time
Why has Love got Me losing my mind

He was all things rough
But sometimes
He refined my situation

He was brown skin and brown eyes
Beauty personification

He was my dream
My fantasy
My needs were met in his smile
He was everything I needed him to be

I could melt away in his smile
And one day, I did

I melted right out of his fucked-up life!

MARGIE

Chubby
Light-skinned
Talented
Teacher's pet
Two thick black pigtails
Wavy hair smoothed by water and lotion
Eyes bright and brown
Asking questions adults don't want to answer
Hugs and kisses to Mama's cheeks
Singing and shining
Growing more
Afraid of the world
Bullied
No pants allowed
Only dresses and skirts
Strange confinement
When climbing a jungle gym
She grows older
Reaching out for something
That makes it all clearer
For years
She won't know what is real

NOURISHMENT

Poisonous thought
Greed refined
Laced with hatred
Deteriorate
The will to live

Learning lies
burned into memory
Vast trenches carved into truths
That never existed

Evil allowed to rule
While growing in our silence
Marbling into our speech
Stealing away questions

Denying us as unreasonable
Flesh cut from bone
No longer grows,
The soul expands
beyond mortality

Still, we endure

CONSTRUCT

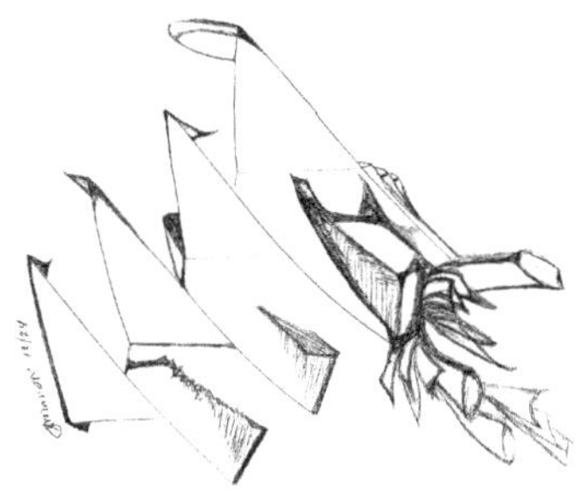

Skin folds and creases at the corners of my
mouth
Pulled back in a grimace of anger born out of
fear
Laughter erupting from confusion
Cemented with willful ignorance

But

My lips release words of love
Unleash sounds of protection
Hold back thoughts of cruelty

Feet spread beneath my weight,
Carry me toward destinations
I don't belong
Stone in my heart softens to lava

Defiant acceptance
I am here to live

10

MMMMMMM

Softness pressed between tongue and lip
Buttery slip
Sugary grit
Syrupy residue
Firm and plump
In my grip

Oasis in the fleshiness of my cheek
Drenching my mouth
With rivers of sweet
Rivulets dribble down my chin
Fruit of love
Kiss

SUBMERGED

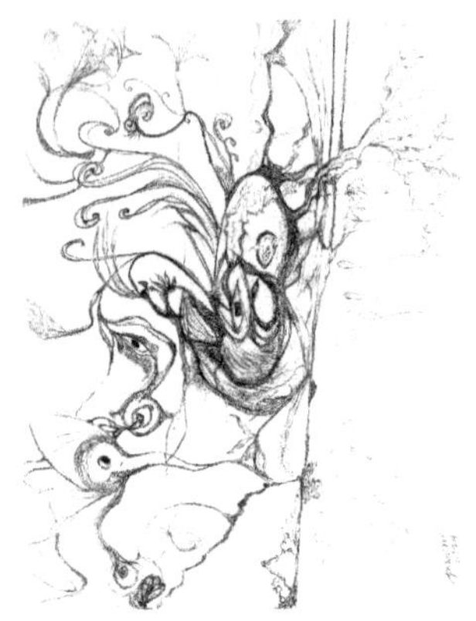

In the absence of touch
Beauty of loneliness
Comforts me
I swim in the greenish blues
Like the Aegean sea
Paralysis from fear
Knowing truths that
Leave me hollow
Hear
Listen
With desire
To save
To heal
To give

Disappear
Until it ends

Let's go again

THE SLAP

Gut-wrenched
Flushed skin

Tiny hairs raised on my neck
Water fills my mouth

Eyes stinging
Tears

Overflowing agony
Mind flooded

Thoughts of revenge
Memories cemented

Your hand never
Touched my face

BIG MAMA

In your house.
I was home.
At my house.
I felt alone.

Mama had to work
'Cause Daddy couldn't hold a job

I was dropped off with you at
Six weeks old

A house filled with dark-skinned children
Fed and loved

The other children would grow up and leave,
I always stayed behind

Now I can see it's because Mama wasn't
always right

You taught us to pledge allegiance
to a flag
I wished you had taught us poems instead

We learned numbers and ABCs, played
outside, had good food to eat.

Homemade cakes and buttermilk cornbread
made from scratch.

Your house was immaculate, not like ours
A huge glass-paned window in the front
Let the Christmas tree shine

Because of your kindness, I got to see New
York for the first time

You made me your family
I wish I had known how much you loved me

I wish I had been there when you took your
last breath

I will be forever grateful for your presence
Your love helped me build strength

TALENT

Barely out of diapers
Mesmerizing adults
Potential
Star
She could go very far
Will she?

Letting the world
Raise her little girl
Afraid in her religious shell
Maybe her baby
Has been chosen
Just pray the fear away
What God has in store for

Acceptance followed by rejection
Talented
Lazy and crazy
Throw money in her life
But keep guidance to a minimum

"Mama, I don't want to go anymore"
"Baby, you're so close"

Close to what?

Talent is only a gift
If exchanged with love

When ignored
It's suffocation

JOKE

Doubled over
Trembling with sound
I pull away from grief
I am not here long
Endlessness of brevity
Grabbing moments of escape
While I stare into the day
Blinking myself into consciousness

The tickle in the back of my throat
Is a gift from beyond
I embody levity
Healing
That makes my mouth water
With desire

These are times that make me crave peace
Children napping, embraced, comforted

EASE

Eyes open in silence
Body heavy in comfort
Softness touching skin
Breathing deep
Slumber enveloping limbs
Burrow under blankets
Fifteen minutes on each side
Until I'm done
Buried in warmth
Drifting into a series of dreams

ANJOLI

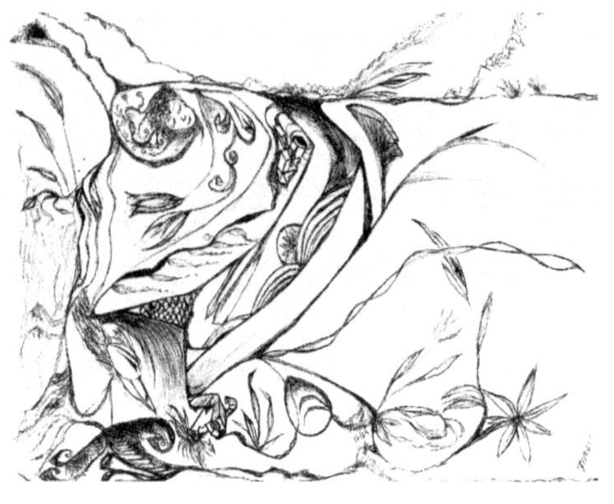

We walked through the woods
Looking for adventure

Running in the field
Kicking a soccer ball back and forth

Watching you on the playground
Trying to make friends
My heart broke

I played with you when they wouldn't

Cushioning the sting of rejection

Always wanted
Just unexpected

We have that in common

I drank too much
Numbing my own pain

Neglected

I let you down
I will never forget

I don't expect your forgiveness
You will always have my love

KATRINA

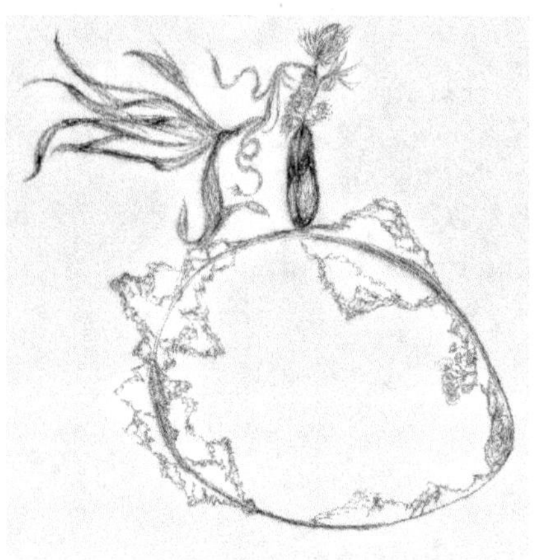

At one and a half, flat-footed
you looked up at the table

You stood in front of the television
Luciano Pavarotti held your attention

You started climbing chairs
As soon as you could stand

We watched the world panic
While we watched you learn to laugh

Endless love for you
More than a little fear

What's the best way
To raise a baby girl

Would we be good enough to ourselves
So we could be better for her?

Now halfway to ten
You already have opinions

The lines are getting fuzzy
Who is raising who here?

CHRIS

In a spiraling, blinding storm
I walked backward in my life
Only ever reaching the beginning
Over and over again

Never had a compass
Familiar with failure self-destruction
Settling for physical companionship
When intimacy was the desire

Bustello in our mugs
Walking through the patch of green
Across from the rundown apartments
where we met

I invited you to the play I was in–
You were so nervous
You drank bleach by mistake
And showed up anyway
Sitting in the audience watching

You rode a bike then
In Sarasota, Florida
You cooked in kitchens then
And entertained rude Russians

You expressed your longing for me then
And would rescue me from a bad decision

You have been more than a lover
More than a friend

You have been my life preserver

ARNAB

What were we anyway?
It wasn't your fault
My craving for your attention.
I had issues
But I couldn't see you had some too.
Tolerated me
or was it love?
I don't regret loving you.
I just wish it had been briefly, from a distance
In your eyes, I see pain.
I'm sure I caused more than a little.
The dogs, the cats, the hoarding.
I always saw your potential.
You made a way for yourself in this world
that kicked you down so many times
I am impressed with your resilience
I know it helped build mine

MAMA OLIVIA

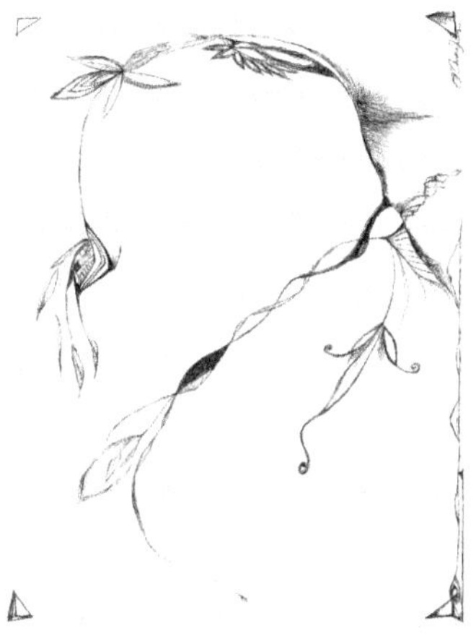

Late-night praise sessions
Speaking in tongues
Dancing in the Spirit
Shaking off the devil

Ignoring sexuality
Remembering your rare smile
Prayer circles in the middle of our
government housing
Preaching anywhere you felt like
MARTA buses, in churches, on the street
corner in Downtown

That long walk down Fairburn Road in the
dark
When we had no car
You couldn't hold your bowels
Something you ate did you wrong
I stood and waited for you to relieve yourself
on that rock
that seemed to appear just for that purpose

"We never know the day or the hour
We must pray the Lord give us power
Strength in this cold, cruel world
Margie, we're praising the Lord now. Stop all
that laughing."

What did you think near the end?
I bathed you
Cleaned you after to toileting
You put your head on my shoulder like a child

It is my turn to care for you
Prepare you for your next big journey

DADDY GEORGE

31

Mama said I walked like you
I wouldn't know

47

There were more lightning bugs then
When I was a girl

Maybe I stopped paying attention
Or is the world covering up the marvel?

Dixie Hills where Granddaddy bought land
with an eight-grade education

Fulton County Grady baby
Martin Luther King Junior was more than
just a street name

Six Flags over Georgia was just a good time
I didn't know the hateful history

We screamed on rollercoasters
that took my breath away

We emptied Mama's pocketbook
While she prayed to make rent

MARTA
(Moving Africans Rapidly Through Atlanta)
Was our way around the city

Mama had the monthly pass
We shared it as a family

Every neighborhood had a corner store
Mostly owned by Koreans

Paradise Academy
Margaret Mitchell Elementary

Sutton Middle
Then Westminster

We lived in the house Granddaddy built
With an eighth-grade education I was two
years old in that house

When I pulled the steam iron down on my leg

Forty-seven years gone

The scar is faint
still there

9 789367 399583